# Moving with Ease and Confidence

## A Simple Step-by-Step System

# Synopsis

MOVING WITH EASE AND CONFIDENCE DIVIDES MOVING INTO THREE PHASES, EACH OF WHICH CONTAINS A SERIES OF IMPORTANT INDIVIDUAL STEPS.

FOLLOWING THESE STEPS IS A LITTLE LIKE USING A GPS. THEY WILL GET YOU TO YOUR DESIRED DESTINATION MORE EASILY AND WITH CONSIDERABLY LESS ANXIETY AND STRESS.

# Phase One

## STEPS 1 through 4

# The Emotional Part of Moving

This phase sets the stage for your move by encouraging you to:

- Consider Your Focus
- Create a New-Home Vision
- Make a Moving and Settling-In Planner
- Challenge Your Moving Beliefs

# Phase Two
## STEPS 5 through 8

# The Physical Part of Moving

This phase empowers you to:

- Sort Your Belongings by Category
- Identify Your Storage Needs

- Use Floor and Furniture Arrangement Plans
- Pack with Unpacking in Mind

## Phase Three
### STEPS 9 through 12

### The Completion Part of Moving

This phase helps you to:

- Use a Change of Address Notification List
- Prepare for Your Moving Day
- Make Your Moving Day Orderly and Organized
- Create a Comfortable and Welcoming New Home

While each of us needs the shelter of a roof above our heads, moving from one home and into another is a conscious choice!

It's a choice which requires courage and the desire to live in surroundings that satisfy our emotional as well as our physical needs.

This book is written to support you in fulfilling that desire and to guide you in making your move a rewarding prelude to a possibility-filled new part of your life.

Gail Van Kleeck, Author of MOVING WITH EASE AND CONFIDENCE and President of Dover Interiors Inc.

# Moving with Ease and Confidence

## A Simple Step-by Step System

# by Gail Van Kleeck
## Author, Moving Specialist, and Interior Designer

**Bringing the Magic of Possibility into
Your Home and Your Life**

ISBN-13: 978-0692653876
ISBN-10: 0692653872

Gail Van Kleeck
      Moving with Ease and Confidence: A Simple
      Step-by-Step System

Moving
      Moving with Ease and Confidence: A Simple
      Step-by-Step System
      by Gail Van Kleeck

Editor/Proof Reader: Barbara Anderson
"I'm Write for You"
Phone: (502) 533-8937
Email: barbara.anderson@twc.com

Book Design, Layout, and Format: Connie Dunn
Publish with Connie
(http://publishwithconnie.com)
Email: connie@publishwithconnie.com
Phone: (508) 446-1711

**Bringing the Magic of Possibility into Your Home and Your Life**

# Table of Contents

# Introduction

**There is an emotional as well as a physical component of moving, but the emotional component is all too frequently ignored.**

While I promise to give you countless SIMPLE and LOGICAL suggestions for making the physical part of your move easier, FOCUSING FIRST ON THE EMOTIONAL PART WILL MAKE IT A MORE POSITIVE AND REWARDING EXPERIENCE!

\*\*\*

Before I begin, I'd like to tell you a short story about a couple who took their two young children on a camping vacation.

The four of them were riding their bikes along a path in the woods when they came upon a sign that read "Naturalist Center."

Just as the father was thinking how nice it would be for his children to see examples of plants and animals indigenous to the area, three completely naked bikers pedaled past them.

"How am I going to explain that to my children?" he wondered. Then his thoughts were interrupted by his oldest son.

"Hey Dad, did you see that?" the six year old shouted. "They weren't wearing their helmets."

\*\*\*

I love this story because it's clean and funny and also because it so perfectly illustrates that **WHAT WE FOCUS ON IS WHAT WE SEE.**

# Phase One

## The Emotional Part of Moving

# Consider Your Focus

## STEP ONE

**A paradigm is something we believe to be true and most paradigms about making a move contain the belief that it will be overwhelming and stressful.**

Focusing on this negative paradigm can make it nearly impossible to imagine making a move in an orderly, organized manner or the freedom, flexibility and limitless possibilities a new home may offer.

Despite what many of us believe, it has been scientifically proven that our brain can only focus fully on one thing at a time. This means every moment we spend thinking thoughts that cause us to feel anxious or fearful is a moment in which we are unable to see and embrace more positive, empowering possibilities.

**Just as choosing to focus on what is positive and possible can substantially improve the quality of your life, choosing to change this negative moving paradigm can vastly improve the quality of your move.**

THE BEST WAY TO MAKE THAT VERY IMPORTANT CHANGE IS TO FOCUS FIRST ON CREATING A NEW-HOME VISION.

# Create a New-Home Vision

## STEP TWO

**The New-Home Vision You Create will make EVERY Moving Decision Easier.**

Your new-home vision will become an empowering part of your entire move. It will support you in the emotional phase, help you make better moving decisions in the moving phase and be the core of how successfully and happily you settle in.

**It is important to do the suggested writing in this step.**

Your responses don't need to be long, but there is something about writing that will slow you down just enough to give you better insights and empower you to make your moving decisions with greater clarity.

Using three-ring paper, write your answers to The Seven Successful Moving Questions:

## THE SEVEN SUCCESSFUL MOVING QUESTIONS

1. Why are you planning to move?
2. What do you hope will change once you have moved and settled in?
3. Think about the person you were when you moved into your current home. What has changed for you since then?
4. How have those changes affected who you are and what you need from your new home?
5. What was important to you when you moved into your current home?

6. What parts of what you valued then are still important to you now?
7. What would you like to do in your new home that you haven't had the time, the energy or the desire to do until now?

\*\*\*

Using your answers to THE SEVEN SUCCESSFUL MOVING QUESTIONS to guide you, write a brief description of your vision for your new home.

**Don't write about how you would like it to LOOK.** Write instead about how you would like to **USE IT**, how you would like it to **FEEL**, and how it could **SUPPORT and ENRICH THE QUALITY OF YOUR LIFE.**

Be as creative and authentic as you've ever been and don't limit yourself with worries about a budget.

Imagine yourself drawing a beautiful outline of your completed new home so you can fill in the details later on and then dream the fullest and richest dream you can imagine.

\*\*\*

When I moved into a new home more than thirty years ago, I had just come to the end of a long-term marriage, was starting life anew and was frightened, sad and anxious about nearly everything.

What follows is the new-home vision I once wrote for myself. I've included it here in the hope my example will make writing your own new-home vision easier and more fun.

*"I want my home to feel safe and peaceful and healing. I need it to be my haven. I need it to be a place where I feel comfortable and nurtured, where*

*I can go barefoot or sit by the fire and read a book."*

*"I want every room in my new home to encourage genuine conversation."*

*"I need places for the simple things I treasure: my books, that awkward piece of pottery my son made his first year in camp and the paper-mache' angel my sister sculpted for me one Christmas."*

*"I would like my home to be a place where I can feel happy when I'm alone. I also want it to be a simple, straightforward, honest and gentle place that welcomes spontaneous moments and where love and laughter can make their presence known."*

*"I need a kitchen with room enough to encourage those who would like to help and a well-stocked pantry to give me the feeling of abundance."*

*"I need my home to be a place where people can dance in the kitchen or sing around the piano, a place they look forward to returning to and feel reluctant to leave."*

Happily for me, the new-home vision I created so long ago became a reality over time. So now I encourage you to begin writing one of your own.

*** 

Throughout the more than thirty years I'd lived in my home I'd helped countless clients with their move. Then just as I was writing MOVING WITH EASE AND CONFIDENCE, I made the decision to move myself...this time to somewhat smaller surroundings.

That decision affected the content of this book and inspired me to share what I have learned through personal experience as well as through the experiences of others.

It also meant that I needed to review and revise my answers to the seven questions and to write an entirely different new-home vision as a prelude to my move.

Taking time to do those two things helped me leave the home I had loved for so long and freed me to look forward to my new home with optimism and faith.

*** 

When I was in the midst of my recent move I did something I had never asked a client to do. Noticing how overwhelmed I was feeling with my seemingly endless "moving-to-do list," I began jotting down daily notes to remind myself of the progress I'd already made.

The results were worth the effort! My moving notes helped me stay focused on what I had already accomplished and kept me from using my precious time and energy worrying about what I still needed to do.

Since it made such a difference for me, I am sharing some of my daily observations with you in the hope they will inspire you to celebrate your personal progress by making notes of your own.

*February 13: The goal for selling our home is to make it look as though its new family could see themselves moving into it without making any major changes. Paul, the home improvement contractor, started work today. He is going to paint the walls and ceilings and I am going to paint the woodwork. All is well. All is well.*

*February 15: Paul had a conversation with me about painting the woodwork. He says he has seen the level of my painting expertise and doesn't want my workmanship to diminish the quality of his. We have* negotiated a price for HIM to paint woodwork too. Honestly, when I think of how much of it there is, I'm relieved. All is well. All is well.

March 18: We are getting closer and closer to the time we will be moving. I have been drawing floor and furniture arrangement plans so we will have a clearer sense of what we can bring with us and what may need to be replaced. The charity I called came today and picked up twelve bags of things we don't really need. Parker, my dear life partner, wants to keep our hideous but comfortable living room sofa. Otherwise we are great. There is so much to think about. All is well. All is well.

April 12: We are replacing our old living room sofa with a beautiful blue-gray sectional. Parker is alright with that because we are also getting a larger TV. ☺ All is well. All is well.

# Make a Moving and Settling-In Planner

## STEP THREE

There are so many things to consider when you are moving and having a MOVING and SETTLING-IN PLANNER will keep you from worrying about forgetting something important.

Begin by buying a good quality 2 inch, three-ring notebook to use as your *Moving and Settling-In Planner*. You will also need:

- Several packages of subject divider tabs
- A pack of three-ring paper
- Scissors
- Some pens and pencils
- A roll of double-sided tape

Put the subject divider tabs in your binder and add these subjects in the following order:

- Your answers to the seven successful moving questions
- The new-home vision you wrote
- Your daily moving accomplishments notes
- Existing furniture measurements
- Potential future purchases
- A subject tab for each of your new home's rooms
- Moving costs and related information
- An appointment calendar
- Contact and source information
- New address notifications

Feel free to insert any additional categories that meet your specific needs and then put your contact information on the inside of the front cover so it can be returned to you if you happen to lose it.

**The best time to begin making your Moving and Settling-In Planner is the moment you begin thinking of making a move.**

Beginning with what you already have is an important part of both the physical and settling-in phases of your move.

Measuring the pieces of furniture you currently own is important. It will give you a better sense of what you are able to use in your new home and what you may need to replace.

Work on filling in the information for as many subject divider tabs as you can. If you haven't found your new home yet, fill in as much as you can and then complete what remains once you've chosen a home.

When your Moving and Settling-In Planner is complete you will have all the information you will need to make your move easier and more orderly and organized than you can imagine.

**The more details you add to your Moving and Settling-In Planner the more helpful and important it will become.**

# Challenge Your Moving Beliefs

## STEP FOUR

There are countless paradigms related to the physical part of moving and all of them are worth questioning. While they may contain an element of truth they are basically based on our focus and on the way we choose to see and experience our move.

One of the paradigms, or common beliefs, about moving to smaller surroundings is that you need to focus on GETTING RID OF AS MANY OF YOUR BELONGINGS AS POSSIBLE.

**You can change that negative paradigm simply by choosing to focus on KEEPING ONLY THE THINGS THAT HOLD PRECIOUS MEMORIES, MAKE**

**YOU HAPPY OR ARE TRULY NECESSARY AND USEFUL.**

Think for a moment about the power of words and phrases and how they affect your beliefs and actions. Phrases such as "getting rid of" or "throwing out" can make you feel anxious or even embarrassed and defensive about clinging so tightly to material things.

**You can change that paradigm by choosing to see yourself as a generous person who wants more freedom, less responsibility and fewer things to weigh you down. You can also change it by seeing yourself as someone who welcomes the possibility of living a simpler, less cluttered and more peaceful life.**

Another paradigm that needs changing is the commonly held belief that the best way to prepare for a move is to focus on sorting your belongings one room or closet or drawer at a time.

**In truth, the best way to prepare for a move is to sort your belongings by category.**

*** 

Imagine that one of your categories is pencils. If you go through your pencils one room or one drawer at a time, you are likely to pack more pencils than you need because you have no idea of how many pencils you actually have.

Now imagine going through your desk drawer, your purse, the junk drawer in your kitchen, the cabinet beside the telephone and the table beside your favorite chair collecting all the pencils you can find.

Then imagine putting them on your kitchen table and sorting through all of them at once.

When you see all of your pencils together you will be less likely to worry about not having enough and more likely to choose only the ones you will actually need.

Although pencils are items with very little emotional attachment, they are a symbol of all your other belongings.

**Dividing your belongings into categories and choosing only the things you love and need can empower you to live a simpler, less cluttered and more peaceful feeling life.**

# Phase Two

## The Physical Part of Moving

# Sort Your Belongings by Category

## STEP FIVE

**Begin your sorting by focusing first on these three MAJOR CATEGORIES:**

- Artwork
- Books
- Decorative Accessories

## Category One
### Artwork

Walk through the rooms in your home and pause in front of each piece of artwork on your walls and then ask yourself just one question: **"IS THIS SOMETHING I WANT TO WAKE UP TO AND ENJOY EVERY DAY FOR THE REST OF MY LIFE?"**

If your answer is "YES" put a sticker or post-it on it and move on to the other artwork on your walls as well as the pieces you've stored in your basement or attic.

**The pieces of artwork you choose to bring with you when you move usually have several important things in common:**

1. You loved them the moment you saw them and have a story to tell about them.
2. They hold memories of places or people who are precious to you or remind you of places you have visited or would still like to see.
3. Their total function in your life is simply to make you smile.

**The pieces of artwork you can let go of with relative ease usually have several other things in common:**

1. They were given to you as a gift and you hung them because you didn't want to seem unappreciative.
2. *You had an empty wall to fill and bought a pleasing piece of artwork to fill it.*
3. They are something you once liked and have outgrown, or they don't reflect or relate to the way you would like your new home to feel.

\*\*\*

**With the exception of artwork, most MAJOR CATEGORIES of belongings can be divided into MINOR CATEGORIES. These MINOR CATEGORIES can then be divided into SUB-CATEGORIES.**

If that seems confusing this may help:

1. Kitchen contents are a MAJOR CATEGORY.

2. Most MAJOR CATEGORIES can be divided into MINOR CATEGORIES.
3. One of the MINOR CATEGORIES of Kitchen Contents is dishes.
4. Serving dishes and dishes from which you eat are both SUB-CATEGORIES of dishes.

***

Category Two

## Books

Choose the room in your home that contains most of your books and set up a card table there. Bring all the books from the rest of your home into that room and use the card table for sorting.

Fiction and Non-Fiction books are both MINOR BOOK CATEGORIES. Some of the SUB-CATEGORIES of

Fiction are books about romance, adventure or mystery.

Some of the SUB CATEGORIES of Non-Fiction are biographies, auto-biographies and self-help books.

Once you have sorted your books into SUB-CATEGORIES ask yourself these three questions:

1.  Is this a book I once loved and would like to re-read?
2.  Is this a book I would like to loan or give to a friend?
3.  Will I use this as a reference book or would I prefer to do my research electronically?

Put the books you've chosen to keep into small boxes, such as the boxes used for wine, then label each box with the following information:

- The room from which these books were taken

- The SUB-CATEGORY of these books
- The room in which you plan to put them

Put the books you've decided not to keep in heavy duty paper bags with handles and take them to a library or a charity of your choice.

\*\*\*

**If you are planning to move bookcases from your current home to your new home, the following four steps will make unpacking your books much easier:**

1. Sort your books by SUB-CATEGORIES and arrange the SUB-CATEGORIES together in your bookcases.
2. Label each shelf in each bookcase with a different number.

3. Take a photo of each bookcase and its contents.
4. Pack your boxes with your SUB-CATEGORIES together and label the boxes.

For example, your box label might look like this: From: Upper hall bookcase/detective books to: shelf 4/ family room.

***

## Category Three
## **Decorative Accessories**

The MAJOR CATEGORY of decorative accessories can usually be divided into two MINOR CATEGORIES:

- Objects you generally place on tables
- Objects you generally place on shelves

These MINOR CATEGORIES include SUB-CATEGORIES such as sculptures, statues or figurines, vases, candle sticks, decorative pottery, decorative glass, bookends, paper weights, and silk flower arrangements.

Putting just one SUB-CATEGORY at a time on a table will help you sort through them more easily. Simply ask yourself the same question you asked about your artwork.

**"IS THIS SOMETHING I WANT TO WAKE UP TO AND ENJOY EVERY DAY FOR THE REST OF MY LIFE?"**

The good news about sorting your belongings by SUB-CATEGORY is that:

- Your new home will feel less cluttered.
- Your move will be more organized.
- Your belongings will be easier to unpack and put neatly away.
- You will be surrounded by only the things you truly love or need.

The bad news about this kind of sorting is that it can disrupt or create disorder in nearly every room of your home... but there is good news in that bad news.

\*\*\*

What I discovered as I did this myself was the more disorder I temporarily created, the less I grieved leaving the home I had lived in and loved for so long.

\*\*\*

Once you have sorted your artwork, books and accessories, move on to the MAJOR CATEGORIES of clothing and kitchen contents.

**As you continue sorting your belongings you are likely to notice that some of the SUB-CATEGORIES have small SUB-CATEGORIES of their own.**

For example: Clothing is a MAJOR CATEGORY. Footwear is one of the MINOR CATEGORIES of clothing and some of the SUB-CATEGORIES for footwear are sneakers, sandals, dress shoes, black shoes, red shoes and boots….

Boots have small SUB-CATEGORIES of their own, such as snow boots, dress boots, work boots, tall boots and short boots.

**The more specific you are about sorting by individual SUB-**

CATEGORIES the easier it will be to let go of the things you have been holding onto "just in case" and to move into your new home with only the belongings you truly need and love.

# Use Floor
# and Furniture
# Arrangement Plans

## STEP SIX

Quarter-inch scale floor and furniture arrangement plans are VERY IMPORTANT tools for planning what to bring with you. They will also be important in helping you settle comfortably and confidently into your new home.

Floor and furniture arrangement plans will:

- Enhance your new-home vision.
- Help you avoid costly mistakes.
- Show you whether your current sofa will work in your new family room or if a sectional or smaller seating

piece would create a better conversation area.

- Guide you in thinking about creating better storage.
- Show you where to install your overhead lighting.
- Help you determine the best area rug sizes for your individual rooms.
- Make you feel more confident about your new furniture choices.
- Help you see possibilities you may not have noticed.
- Make you want to hug yourself every time you walk through your new home's door.

**Yes, I know. Very few people who are moving want to be bothered with quarter-inch scale floor and furniture arrangement plans... but THEY ARE REALLY IMPORTANT AND YOU NEED THEM!**

While you can measure the walls in your new home as well as the furniture you would like to bring with you, it's difficult to imagine how the individual pieces will work together without using quarter-inch-scale furniture arrangement plans.

It's hard to overstate the importance of these plans and there are several options for obtaining them.

## Option One

**You can search the internet for interior designers in your area and then interview several of them by phone.**

- Tell them you need quarter-inch scale floor plans of the rooms in your new home and guidance in using them to creating furniture arrangement plans.

- If you have been given a quarter-inch scale architectural plan of your new home, the designer you call can use it to create the furniture arrangement plans for your individual rooms.

- If you have been given a plan that fits comfortably onto a regular size sheet of copy paper, the interior designer you call may need to enlarge it to quarter-inch scale before guiding you with your arrangement plans.

- Ask the designers you call how they charge, how they work with clients and if they would help you work with what you already have.

- Then ask if they will guide you in purchasing new furniture if what you already have doesn't satisfy your needs.

- Listen to your instincts and notice which of the designers seems the best informed and makes you feel the most at ease.

## Option 2

**You can ask a friend who is good at details to help you.**

## Option 3

**You can purchase my e-book, THE MAGICAL INTERIOR DESIGN GUIDE, which is a companion to MOVING WITH EASE AND CONFIDENCE.**

It is filled with easy-to-implement guidance, including the simple steps for making your own floor and furniture arrangement plans. It also contains quarter-inch scale furniture templates you can copy and use.

You can find the ordering information at the back of this book.

\*\*\*

**Moving to different surroundings is, in many ways, like beginning a fresh new part of your life.**

Even if your budget keeps you from purchasing the few new pieces of furniture you would like right away, having a furniture arrangement plan will keep you from making costly "moving-in mistakes" and give you something to save for and enjoy using later on.

# Consider Your Storage

## STEP SEVEN

No matter how beautifully your rooms are arranged or how comfortable and inviting they feel, if they don't have adequate storage they won't fully serve your needs.

Because storage is so important, my decorating e-book, THE MAGICAL INTERIOR DESIGN GUIDE, devotes an entire chapter to creating storage in every room. The following additional suggestions are possibilities you may also wish to consider:

## Suggestion One
If one of your rooms has a wall without windows you can build-in or buy enough twenty-four-inch deep cabinets, or bookcases with doors, to

cover as much of your windowless wall as possible.

Make sure what you choose has adjustable shelving and buy several extra shelves.

Measure the length and width of one of the shelves and then go to a store that has a good selection of plastic containers.

Look for storage containers that are just a little shorter and a little narrower than the shelves so they will slide in and out as though they were drawers.

The optimal height for these "container-drawers" is from seven to ten inches depending on what you plan to store.

## Suggestion Two

You can use small containers placed on shelves as drawers in your kitchen and bathroom base cabinets or in almost any other storage piece that has shelving.

Storing your belongings in drawers is more efficient than stacking them on shelves because drawers allow you to use all of your available space, while stacked items usually leave an unused space above them.

## Suggestion Three

If your space is limited look for vertical storage such as tall furniture, bookcases and narrow armoires or cabinets.

## Suggestion Four

Consider using a decorative shelf in some of your rooms so you can display the belongings you love without cluttering your table tops.

## Suggestion Five

Repurpose your existing furniture by using it in unusual ways. Think about using a long bedroom bureau as a console on which to place your family room TV. You could also put it on short legs, paint it and use it as your dining room server.

## Suggestion Six

Drape a patterned fabric over a sturdy box which is slightly lower than your sofa's arm and use it as an end table beside the sofa. Put magazines or paperwork in a flat basket and slide it under the fabric skirt for easy to access storing.

*** 

My former mother-in law declined our offer to live with us for a while because she said she couldn't possibly live in a home with such poor housekeeping.

In truth, our home was always reasonably clean, but it was also sometimes cluttered. While at the time I was offended by her statement, I took it to heart and began looking for ways to create better storage. This is what I found:

**If there is a place in every room for everything that needs to be stored and used in that room, there is always the possibility that sooner or later those things will be put away.**

# Pack with Unpacking in Mind

## STEP EIGHT

**Before anyone tapes your moving boxes shut be sure each box is labeled on ALL FOUR SIDES AS WELL AS THE TOP.**

Correctly labeled boxes can make a HUGE and DRAMATIC DIFFERENCE in the ease with which you complete your move.

It is often necessary for movers to pile boxes on top of one another. If your labels are on the sides of your boxes as well as the top, you'll be able to find the ones you need more easily.

If each of your labels contain the following specific information you will substantially simplify your unpacking:

- The room and the place in that room from which the contents were taken
- The SUB-CATEGORY of the box's contents
- The room and place in that room where you would like the box's contents to be unpacked.

***

**Specific labeling is especially important when you are unpacking and putting away the contents of a kitchen.**

While the following suggestions may seem like extra work you will thank me when you are unpacking.

## Kitchen Drawers and Cabinets

Before you begin sorting the contents of your existing kitchen ask permission to go into your new home to take measurements and photographs of your kitchen storage areas.

Bring the following items with you:

- A measuring tape
- A few pens or pencils
- A package of post-its
- A camera or a cell phone with a camera
- Your Moving and Settling-In Planner

Put a post-it on each of your new kitchen's cabinets and drawers and then:

- Write a different letter of the alphabet on each of the post-its.
- Take measurements of each space.
- Take a photo of each space.
- Put this information in your Moving and Settling-In Planner.

When you are labeling your kitchen boxes, use the letters you placed on your new home's kitchen cabinets and drawers to indicate where the contents of each box should be placed.

While you may want to rearrange some parts of your kitchen later, using specific category information on your labels as well as on the storage areas in your new kitchen will assure that this important room will be basically organized rather than arbitrarily unpacked.

**EVERY MINUTE YOU SPEND LABELING YOUR BOXES WITH THIS SPECIFIC INFORMATION WILL SAVE YOU HOURS OF HEADACHES LATER ON.**

\*\*\*

# Your New Home's Other Storage Spaces

Once you've completed labeling your kitchen drawers and cabinets, walk through the other rooms in your home and look for closets, cabinets, shelving and any other places that could be used for storage.

Take measurements and photos of each of these places and the rooms or spaces in which they are located and then write that information in your Moving and Settling-In Planner.

Having this information will give you the opportunity to plan ahead so you can have specific storage places for everything you need to store.

**One of the benefits of specific labeling is that it facilitates faster and more orderly unpacking so you can relax and begin enjoying your new surroundings sooner.**

There is another huge benefit of paying attention to and measuring all of your new home's potential storage places.

**Having a clearer sense of how much storage space you will actually have can empower you to make better decisions about which belongings you choose to bring with you.**

# Phase Three

## Moving Day and Settling In

# Use a Change of Address Notification List

## STEP NINE

**Whether you are moving across the country or just across town you need to notify your friends, family and the businesses and organizations who serve you about your change of address.**

Happily, the U.S. Post Office will forward your mail so you don't need to create additional stress by attempting to send all of these notifications at once.

Happily too, the post office flags the letters they forward to you with a YELLOW STICKER. This means you will be reminded of whom you still need to notify.

As with your other sorting, it will be easier if you sort your moving notification announcements by category.

The following alphabetized categories will help you:

- Animal care givers
- Banks and financial service providers
- Close friends and family members
- Clubs and organizations
- Credit card services
- Health related organizations and doctors
- Household services
- Government agencies
- Magazines and newspapers
- Utilities

Put these categories in your Moving and Settling-In Planner and leave enough space between them to enter the contact information for the individuals and businesses associated with that category.

**Keeping your address change notification categories in your Moving Planner will give you peace of mind and allow you to send out most of those notifications after you have moved.**

# Prepare for Moving Day

## STEP TEN

### Two Weeks Before Your Move

The two weeks before moving day are especially important because the actions you take in those two weeks can affect the ease with which you move as well as how quickly you settle in.

The following two suggestions will empower you to move into your new home with more ease and confidence:

- Designate one of the lesser-used main-floor rooms in your new home as your temporary box storage and set-up area.
- Ask for help and assign clear and specific tasks.

\*\*\*

# The Temporary Box Storage and Set-Up Room

Designating one of your lesser-used main-floor rooms as a temporary box storage and set-up area is important. Being surrounded by unpacked or partially unpacked boxes throughout your home can keep you from appreciating and enjoying it.

**Your new home's temporary box-storage and set-up area will be used for boxes that NEED IMMEDIATE UNPACKING.**

This includes boxes filled with:

- Artwork
- Lamps and lampshades
- Large accessories
- Artificial flowers or plants
- Bedding and linens

These items are typically packed in larger boxes which take up more physical space. Unpacking these boxes, flattening them and getting them out of your new home as soon as possible will substantially reduce the disorder and confusion of your move.

Your temporary box storage and set-up area will also be used for the boxes that CAN WAIT TO BE UNPACKED.

The contents of these boxes may include:

- Decorative accessories
- Books
- Photos, photo albums and frames
- Home-office supplies

Once you've settled into your space, you can take one box at a time from the temporary box storage and set-up area and then unpack its contents and put them away more leisurely.

*** 

# Create a Moving Team

Ask five friends or family members to be a part of your moving-team and be specific about what you need from them.

This will give them the opportunity to participate in the very courageous transition you are undertaking and also the fulfilling feeling of helping someone they care about.

## Your Moving Team Members

### The Personal Unpacker (one person)

This person will be in charge of opening your wardrobe boxes, putting their contents away and then flattening the empty boxes.

You can also ask them to open and put away the contents of boxes containing shoes, handbags, gloves, scarves and other clothing that is typically stored in drawers or on shelves. This will be easy because your specific labeling will guide them in putting each item where you want it.

Your Personal Unpacker will also be responsible for unpacking and putting away the towels and linens as well as for making the beds.

## The Kitchen Unpackers
## (two people)

These team members will take care of unpacking your kitchen boxes and putting their contents away.

The alphabetical letters you wrote on the boxes containing your kitchen contents and the corresponding letters you taped to your new home's kitchen cabinets and drawers will make it easier for your Kitchen Unpackers to set up your kitchen in the way you would like to use it.

Once they have unpacked the boxes, they can fill some of them with packing paper, flatten the ones that remain and take them out of the kitchen.

## The Hostess with-the-Mostest (one person)

This is the person who will take care of providing food and "music-to-work-by" for the movers and your team. She will also help the other team members by carrying their flattened boxes out of your new home.

Give your Hostess-with-the-Mostest money to purchase an assortment of pre-made salads or cold-cuts, beverages, and paper goods as well as fruit, brownies or other easy-to-eat sweets.

Moving day can be physically challenging for both your team and the movers. If there is a pot of soup simmering on the stove and the evidence of someone providing food, they will be more likely to stay in your home and maintain their momentum.

## The Big Box Director
## (1 person)

The Big Box Director is the person assigned to the temporary box storage and set-up room. They will unpack the boxes that need IMMEDIATE UNPACKING AND GUIDE THE MOVERS IN STACKING THE BOXES THAT DON'T NEED TO BE OPENED IMMEDIATELY.

One of the secrets of settling more effortlessly into your new home is to get the unpacked boxes out of your home as quickly as possible.

# One Week Before Your Move

Because you are familiar with every aspect of your move, assign yourself the title of **Moving Director.**

As the Moving Director, it will be your job to make a copy of each room's furniture arrangement plans as well as the overall furniture arrangement plans for each floor in your new home.

Having these ready to use on the day you move in will help that day to go smoothly.

You will also need to make copies of the job titles and job descriptions for each of your team members. Giving them this information a week or so before you move will allow you to review it with them and respond to their questions and concerns.

**If your team members can see one another's jobs as well as their own**

**they will be more empowered to collaborate and act as a team, which will be fun for everyone.**

Gather together the following moving supplies so you can bring them with you on moving day:

- Masking tape
- Several pens and felt tip markers
- Scissors
- Your Moving and Settling-In Planner
- A box cutter for yourself and one for each of your team members
- Toilet paper for each bathroom
- Several rolls of paper towels
- A spray bottle of Windex or the cleaner of your choice

Plan to bring a bouquet of fresh flowers, a few candles, some matches, paper plates and cups and something festive for your moving team to eat and drink at the end of the day.

**You and your team will be weary but happy at the end of the day and you will be glad you thought of doing something simple and thoughtful to thank them.**

* * *

## The Day Before You Move

Go to your new home the day before you move and bring the following items with you:

- Your moving supplies
- The after-the-move celebration items
- A copy of each room's furniture arrangement plan
- Overall furniture arrangement plans for each floor of your new home

**Tape a copy of each room's furniture arrangement plan to a WINDOW in that room so your movers can see where to place your furniture.**

**Tape copies of the overall furniture arrangement plans for each floor NEAR THE FRONT DOOR where you and the movers can see them.**

This will make it easier for you to show them where to take your furniture and belongings.

The movers will bring your area rugs in first so the furniture can be place on top of them. If you use a few pieces of masking tape to mark the place on the floor where they should be placed, your move will be easier and the movers will be VERY grateful.

If you want your bed or furniture in a specific place, put a piece of masking tape on the wall to show the movers where you would like them to place the CENTER of that furniture.

If you were unable to leave the alphabetical letters you put on your cabinets and drawers when you did your storage measurements, use the photo you took of them to remind you of their placement and tape the correct letters on each cabinet and drawer again.

Once you've completed those tasks, walk to the front door with a confident smile, knowing you have done everything you could to make your moving day as orderly and organized as possible.

*\*\**

## The Night Before You Move

Put the bed linens and pillows for the beds that will be slept in the following night into plastic bags and place your medications and personal care supplies in a small suitcase so you can put them in your car in the morning. This will help your Personal Unpacker to find and take care of them for you.

Then try to get a good night's sleep. If thoughts about the things you need to do are still swirling around in your mind, change your focus by going through the alphabet and thinking about something or someone related to your move, for which you are grateful.

*** 

The night before my recent move I did this myself. It was amazing how peaceful it made me feel. Before I reached the letter M, I'd fallen fast asleep.

The following things on my gratitude list may help you get started with yours:

- *I am grateful that this move is ALMOST over*
- *I am grateful for my BODY and for the way it let me do almost everything I thought was necessary.*
- I'm grateful for the COMPASSIONATE and CARING people who have helped me......

# Make Moving Day Orderly and Organized

## STEP ELEVEN

Start your day by eating something substantial. Just a cup of coffee isn't enough.

Put the bags of linens and the suitcase you packed the previous night in your car and give your Personal Unpacker the key.

Don't make it necessary for people to search for you. Plan to stand at the front door until the movers become familiar with the layout of your home and your moving team is comfortably unpacking.

As the Moving Director you will be responsible for answering questions and for guiding the movers to specific rooms. This means you will need to pay special attention to the boxes that need to be diverted to the temporary big box and set-up room.

**You also need to help your kitchen unpackers by giving the movers specific directions for the kitchen contents boxes.**

Ask them to place the kitchen-category boxes against the wall in a part of the kitchen that doesn't contain cabinets or counters, such as the area set aside for a breakfast table.

If there is no area like that in your kitchen, ask them to pile the kitchen related boxes along a wall just OUTSIDE the kitchen door.

This will give your kitchen-unpacking team more room to move around and will substantially decrease the time in which they can complete their unpacking.

**If you express your appreciation often and remember to focus on what has already been done you will be more relaxed and more able to contribute to the smooth conclusion of your move.**

* * *

After the movers leave bring out the flowers, light the candles and set your table with the food and drinks you brought with you to thank your team.

**There is a certain blessing about being surrounded with the people who have helped you make this incredible journey to a new home. It will be a very long time until you can close your eyes at night without thinking lovingly and gratefully of them.**

# Create a Comfortable and Welcoming Home

## STEP TWELVE

Once most of your unpacking is completed and you've begun to settle in, you may begin thinking about the small things you can do to make your new home feel more comfortable and welcoming.

Comfortable, welcoming homes all have three things in common:

1. Their rooms have a peaceful feeling of flow and connection.
2. They contain enough contrast and diversity to make them feel interesting and alive.

3. The individual pieces in their rooms have a sense of relationship with one another.

***

## Flow and Connection

The easiest way to create a sense of flow and connection in your home is to use a DECORATING SPRINGBOARD.

**Your Decorating Springboard can be a piece of artwork, a decorative rug, a print fabric, a vase of flowers or anything else you might use in a home that contains a MINIMUM OF FIVE DISTINCTLY DIFFERENT COLORS.**

If you use different combinations of your Decorating Springboard's colors in your individual rooms, your entire home will have an inviting feeling of flow and connection.

***

When I moved into my new home, I looked for a Decorating Springboard that combined warm red and rust and golden colors and just enough cool feeling blues and greens to make it interesting.

I could have reupholstered one of my chairs with a patterned fabric, but instead I found a painting of a French street scene containing all the colors I hoped to use in my home.

As soon as I found the painting, the related combination of its colors fell into place and made all my decorating choices both fun and easy.

\*\*\*

## Contrast and Diversity

The more contrast you include in a room the more alive and interesting it will become.

Just as too much flow in a room can make it feel overly peaceful, too much contrast can make it feel overly busy. Knowing this will make your decorating easier.

If one of your rooms feels too quiet, add a vase of white flowers or create a little more contrast with your artwork.

If one of your rooms feels too busy reduce the amount of contrast in that room.

**CONTRAST CALLS ATTENTION TO ITSELF.**

If you have special furniture, lamps or other belongings in your home, contrasting them with their surroundings will draw your eyes to them first.

**Save contrast for the decorative items you love most.**

Remembering that contrast calls attention to itself, paint your heating elements, plugs and plug covers the same color as your walls so your eyes won't be drawn to them first.

Resist the temptation to add contrast to a room with pillows.....Unless of course the pillows were a gift from your favorite aunt and you want your eyes to be drawn to them the moment you walk in the room.

If you buy differently textured pillows in colors closely related to the color of your sofa, your room will contain the subtle and inviting contrast of textures, but your eyes will be drawn first to the things in the room that are more important and personal than pillows.

***

# Relationship

Comfortable and welcoming homes contain a silent sense of relationship between colors and textures as well as between furniture, lamps, artwork and accessories.

**When you are hanging artwork over a mantle or a table, create a relationship between them by hanging that artwork close to the furniture or mantle below it.**

The goal is to draw your eyes gently from artwork to what is below it so you see the two together rather than noticing a large strip of wall between them.

Resist the temptation to cover your mantle with a row of accessories. If you move your accessories closer to one another, your eyes will see them as a group, which will help you to enjoy them more.

To help you remember this, imagine that your accessories and decorative objects have voices and need to be placed close enough to one another to have a conversation.

# Final Thoughts

*It was surprising to me how quickly I felt at home in my new surroundings. I'd expected to miss my kitchen and back yard and garden...but I didn't.*

*I thought instead of how much I liked the colors in my new home and the way the new furniture I'd purchased blended with the things I have treasured for so long. I also thought about how much I was looking forward to living a simpler life and of all the unknown possibilities that lay ahead.*

*I didn't drive past my old home for several weeks, as though seeing it might break my heart ... but it didn't.*

*There is a part of me that feels somehow disloyal to the dear little purple cottage that had sheltered and served me for so long, but there is another part me that feels completely peaceful, happy and contented in my new surroundings.*

*I wish you great happiness and a rich and fulfilling life in your new home. The most important and precious memories from your past will continue to sustain you....But now it is time to notice and embrace the possibilities that await you and the meaningful new memories you have yet to create.*

*WELCOME HOME*

# The Author

Gail Van Kleeck loves life. She is an often funny, sometimes wise and insightful woman whose peaceful presence makes her a trusted friend and an empathetic listener.

Her writing contains the persistent, loyal, compassionate and wanting-to-make-a-difference values she learned as a child.

It is also a reflection of her seven years as a Hospice volunteer and the way that experience touched and changed her perspective, her relationships, her writing and her nearly forty years as an interior designer.

Gail has written two books related to moving and creating a comfortable, welcoming home as well as two inspirational and motivational books.

Her newest book, I HAVE A STORY TELLER IN MY CLOSET, is a book for children of all ages. It is the first in a new series of books about our perspective and what we value. Other books in this series will be available soon.

While she loves both writing and interior design, the most precious parts of her life are her children and grandchildren and the relationships she has with her family of origin as well as with her extended family of choice. She and her long-term life partner, Parker Babbidge, a jazz musician and wooden sailboat builder, live with their Golden Doodle Katie in Northbridge Massachusetts.

Gail wishes you and those you love a life filled with countless reasons to feel grateful.

# Make Gift Giving Easy by ordering Gail Van Kleeck's other books and CDs

\*\*\*

## HOME FOCUSED BOOKS

**MOVING WITH EASE AND CONFIDENCE: A SIMPLE STEP-BY-STEP SYSTEM**

If you, or someone you know, is planning to move and feeling overwhelmed at the thought, you will be endlessly grateful for this helpful little book which is filled with suggestions and information about sorting your belongings, creating storage, packing with unpacking in mind, preparing for the day of your move and creating more comfortable and welcoming surroundings.

TO ORDER GO TO:
http://gailvankleeck.org/movingwithease andconfidence

\*\*\*

## THE MAGICAL INTERIOR DESIGN GUIDE: IDEAS FOR IMPROVING YOUR INNER SPACES FROM THE HOME DECORATING FAIRY GODMOTHER

This is the companion e-book to MOVING WITH EASE AND CONFIDENCE. If you have ever wished you knew more about combining colors, choosing seated furniture, window treatments, working within your budget, how to hang a grouping of family photos, storage, arranging furniture for conversation and much more you will love The MAGICAL INTERIOR DESIGN GUIDE.

TO ORDER GO TO
www.homedecoratingfairy
godmother.com

\*\*\*

# INSIGHTFUL and INSPIRATIONAL BOOKS

## HOW YOU SEE ANYTHING IS HOW YOU SEE EVERYTHING

A collection of short, tenderly-woven stories about life's ordinary moments and how our focus determines what we see. HOW YOU SEE ANYTHING IS HOW YOU SEE EVERYTHING is an insightful and inspiring little book that is small enough to fit on a bedside table and large enough to change a life.

TO ORDER GO TO:
http://gailvankleeck.org/howyousee
anything

\*\*\*

## SIMPLE WISDOM FOR CHALLENGING TIMES

More than just another book of someone else's thoughts, SIMPLE WISDOM FOR CHALLENGING TIMES combines a list of A-Z observations with questions that make it a powerful tool for self-exploration and personal growth. Opening and reading just one page a day can make a noticeable and meaningful difference in the way you see and live your life.

TO ORDER GO TO:
http://gailvankleeck.org/simplewisdom

\*\*\*

# BOOKS FOR CHILDREN OF ALL AGES

## THERE IS A STORYTELLER IN MY CLOSET

This is a heartwarming tale of a little boy who discovers a kind and magical story teller in his closet. She tells him stories about imaginary people, but the boy suspects they are really about him. THERE IS A STORY TELLER IN MY CLOSET is about love and possibility and changing the way we see. It is a wise, tender and thought-provoking story for children of all ages.

TO ORDER GO TO:-
**http://gailvankleeck.org/thereisa storyteller**

\*\*\*

# COMPANION CDS

## WHAT WE FOCUS ON IS WHAT WE SEE

This CD is a collection of stories from HOW YOU SEE ANYTHING IS HOW YOU SEE EVERYTHING as well as others that are new. The combination of Gail's stories and her calming voice will draw you in and expand your sense of what is possible.

If you would like to feel more positive and peaceful you will want to listen to these stories more than once.

TO ORDER GO TO:
http://gailvankleeck.org/whatwefocuson

***

## IMAGINE WALKING THROUGH YOUR NEW FRONT DOOR

This CD about moving is a companion to MOVING WITH EASE AND CONFIDENCE. It explores the power of creating a vision for your new home and reinforces some of the book's important themes. Listening to this CD will help you make your move with a more positive, confident and open-minded spirit.

TO ORDER GO TO:
http://gailvankleeck.org/interior-decorating/imagine-walking-through-your-new-front-door

\*\*\*

**If you would like to receive announcements when Gail Van Kleeck's new books and CDs become available, contact her at gailvankleeck@gmail.com**

# NOTES

# NOTES

**Bringing the Magic of Possibility into Your Home and Your Life**

Made in the USA
San Bernardino, CA
07 April 2016